SOAR WITH SEGMENTING AND EARLY SPELLING

Fun Activity Ideas for 3-8 Year Olds

By No Worksheets Allowed

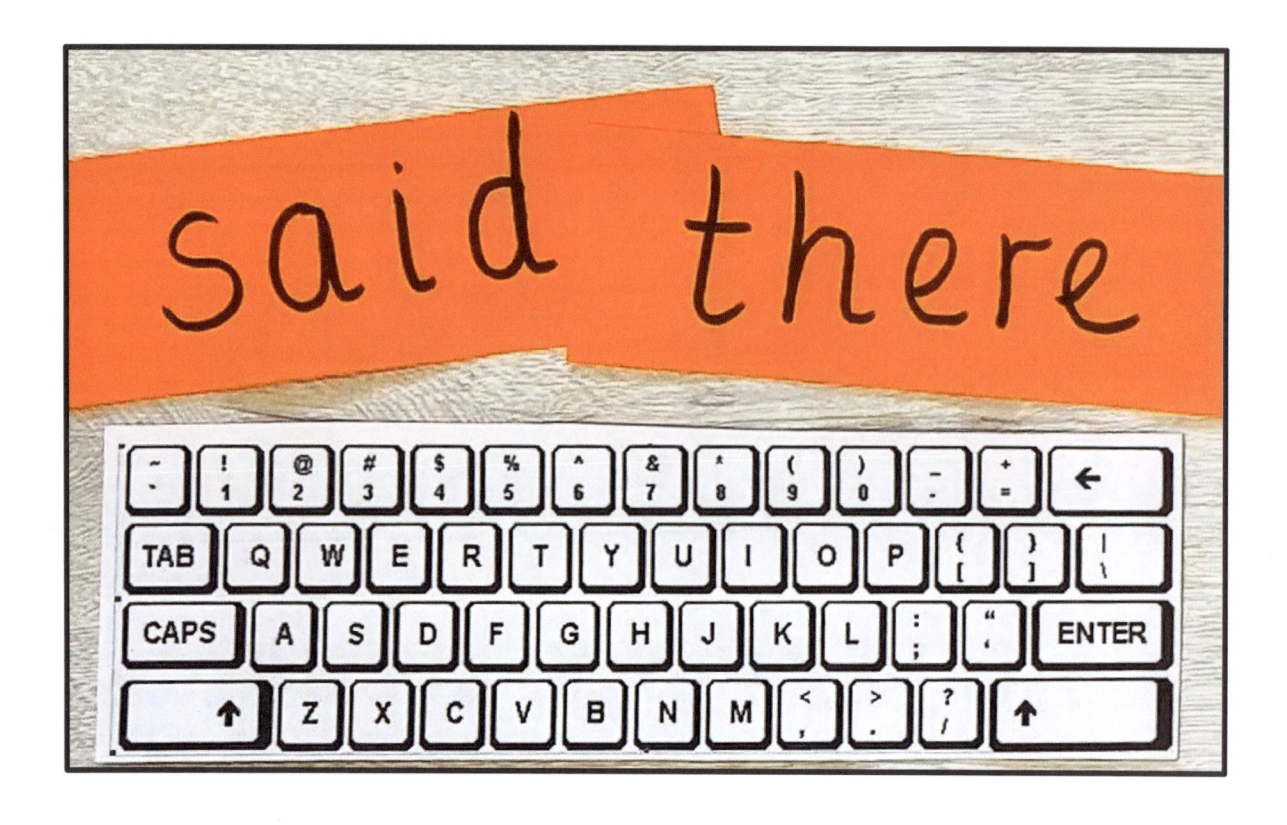

Published by No Worksheets Allowed

© No Worksheets Allowed 2021

All rights reserved. No part of this book may be reproduced or modified in any form, including photocopying, recording or by any information storage and retrieval system, without permission from the publisher.

www.noworksheetsallowed.com

TABLE OF CONTENTS

Introduction	4
What is Phonics?	6
Oral Segmenting Tips	8
Segmenting to Spell Tips	9
Segmenting Activities	10
Tricky Word Spelling Tips	44
Tricky Word Spelling Activities	45

Introduction

I have 17 years teaching experience in a range of U.K. schools, with the vast majority of my time spent in Early Years and Key Stage One. Phonics has always been a passion of mine and I spent a number of years working as phonics' coordinator, driving up standards and ensuring that learning was fun. I have also worked as SENCO and have a wealth of experience in delivering intervention programmes.

After the birth of my third child, I took on a new role as a Teacher Author. Following the success of my first two books, 'Blast Off with Blending' and 'Lift Off with Letters', I couldn't wait to create another title! I love sharing my ideas and making life easier for educators.

The activities contained in this book can be used *alongside* any of the phonics teaching programmes. Each school is able to choose which programme they use and the teaching sequence varies with each one. You should only include the grapheme-phoneme correspondences or common exception words from the appropriate stage in your school's phonics teaching programme.

The aim is to make segmenting fun for children, yet low-prep for parents or educators! The ideas can quickly be put into practice, rather than spending hours preparing resources.

The activities are perfect for teaching individuals and small groups, or to set up as part of your continuous provision. They are ideal for teachers, tutors or parents! Alternatively, they can be used as an intervention to help children who find segmenting and early spelling a struggle. Ideally, an adult should be overseeing the activities to ensure that they are 'firmly focused on intensifying the learning associated with the phonic goal' (Department for Education, April 2021).

The companion store on Teachers Pay Teachers includes extra resources for your phonics lessons, such as downloadable games and activities (plus much more!). You can find it at: www.teacherspayteachers.com/Store/No-Worksheets-Allowed

You can also find me at www.noworksheetsallowed.com.
If you enjoy this book, you might want to take a look at my other two books, **'Blast Off with Blending'** and **'Lift Off with Letters'**. I also have a range of activity books – simply search 'No Worksheets Allowed' (available from Amazon).

What is Phonics?

- **Phonics** is a key strategy in the teaching of reading and spelling. 'Research shows that when phonics is taught in a structured way, starting with the easiest sounds and progressing through to the most complex, it is the most effective way of teaching young children to read.' (Department for Education, 2013).

- Words are made up of sounds, called **phonemes**. A phoneme can be represented by between one to four letters (graphemes), such as 'igh' in l<u>igh</u>t, or 'a' in m<u>a</u>n. Phonics teaches children each of these sounds and how to use them to read and spell.

- **Blending** is when children say the sounds which make up a word (not the letter names) and then merge them together until they can hear what the word is, e.g. c-a-t = cat. The blending of sounds helps children to **decode** unfamiliar or unknown words. Blending plays a very important role in the journey to becoming a fluent reader.

- **Segmenting** is the opposite of blending and teaches children to recognise the segments that form a word. It is when children 'stretch' out a word and then break it up into sounds, e.g. dog = d-o-g. This enables them to spell words.

SEGMENTING TIPS & ACTIVITIES

Oral Segmenting Tips

- Segmenting is the ability to separate a word into its sounds (phonemes). It needs to be taught explicitly, alongside blending.

- A child should **begin with oral segmenting**, i.e. saying the sounds in a word out loud. They don't even need to know what the written letters and sounds (graphemes) look like at this stage.

- Begin by segmenting words made up of two phonemes, such as in (i-n), then three phonemes, such as cat (c-a-t) or shop (sh-o-p), before moving on to longer words. Teach children to listen for the sounds in words by asking them to stretch or chop up the word. They can use their fingers to count the number of sounds which they can hear.

- You should frequently model how to segment a word and encourage children to look carefully at your mouth. This will help them to see the sounds being articulated clearly.

- To orally segment, children need to:
    say the word several times > stretch the word out > say the sounds > put the word back together (blend) to check that they have used the right sounds.

Segmenting to Spell Tips

- Once a child can confidently 'sound out' (orally segment), they can begin to represent the sounds with letters (graphemes).

- The simplest way for children to see the written word is by using magnetic letters. Initially, you can just give them the letters which they will need to make the word.

- Check your school's phonics programme to see which order they teach the sounds in, as this can vary from school to school. You should only focus on the sounds which your child has been taught so that they aren't overwhelmed. For example, if they have been taught s,a,t,p,i,n, they can build words such as in, it, is, sit, etc.

- Once a child is getting to grips with handwriting, they can then begin to write the words.

- Make learning hands-on and engaging by using the activities in this book!

- To segment to spell, children need to:

    say the word several times > stretch the word out > say the sounds > write the sounds down (graphemes) > put the word back together (blend) to check that they have used the right sounds.

Stretchy Segmenting

You Will Need

Rubber bands

Tape

Card

Pen

Scissors

Instructions

- Cut a rubber band so that you have one long piece.
- Cut squares of card and write a grapheme on each to make a word.
- Tape the squares of card onto your rubber band.
- Stretch the word to see which sounds it is made from.

Segmenting Twister

You Will Need

Twister

Pictures

Instructions

- Stick a picture on each circle of the game.
- Spin the spinner and say the word which you put your hand or foot on.
- Segment the word by stretching it out and saying each of its sounds.

Snipping Words!

You Will Need

Strips of paper

Scissors

Pen

Instructions

- Write a word on each strip of paper, e.g. hen.
- Ask the child to blend to read the word and then snip it up to segment the word. Put it back together to check that the word is spelled correctly.
- Repeat with different words.

Puppet Sound Talk

You Will Need

A puppet

Pictures/objects

Alphabet stickers

Paper

Instructions

- Choose a picture or an object.
- Say the word together.
- Use the puppet to demonstrate how to segment the word and identify which sounds it is made from.
- Segment to spell: make the word using alphabet stickers.

Sound Box

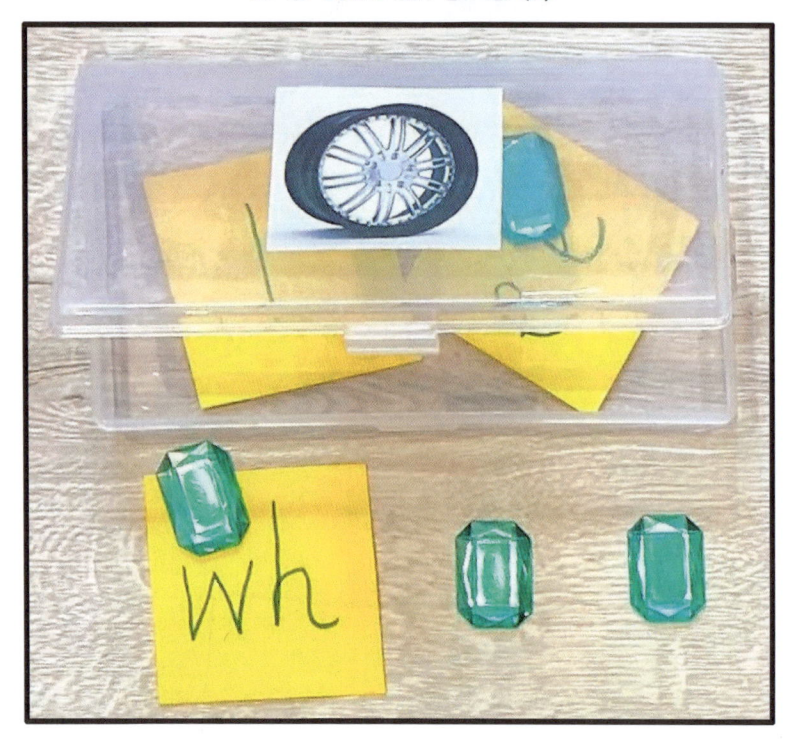

You Will Need

Box

Pictures

Gems/counters

Instructions

- Stick a picture to the outside of the box.
- Say the word together.
- Open the box, take out the 'sounds' (gems) and segment the word, pointing to a gem at a time.
- Segment to spell: put the graphemes needed to make the word inside the box also.

Phonics Phone Messages

You Will Need

Long piece of string

Paper/plastic cups x 2

Pens and paper

Pictures/objects linked to phase which you are working on

Instructions

- Make a hole in the bottom of both cups and thread the string though to make a string telephone. Knot the string to stop it slipping through the cups.
- One child chooses an object in front of them and says the word down the phone.
- The other child listens and breaks the word down into its phonemes. They write them down to spell the word.

Milk the Cow

You Will Need

Rubber glove

String

Sand

Chalk board and chalks

Instructions
- Fill the glove with sand and tie it at the top.
- Say a word to the child.
- The child should pull each 'teat' on the udder (glove) and say the phonemes in the word aloud.
- Segment to spell: write the word on a chalkboard.

Bingo Dabbers

You Will Need

Bingo dabbers

Pictures with sound buttons underneath

Felt pens

Instructions

- Say the word in the picture.
- Use the bingo dabber to dot the sound buttons, saying the phonemes aloud.
- Segment to spell: use felt pens to record the graphemes underneath each sound button.

Playdough Phonics

You Will Need

Playdough

Magnetic letters

Instructions

- Roll the playdough into balls.
- Give each child 3 or 4 balls, depending on how many phonemes the words which you are working on contain.
- Say a word to the children, e.g. goat.
- The children squash their playdough balls as they segment the word, g-oa-t.
- Segment to spell: place magnetic letters underneath each piece of playdough to spell the word.

Karate Segmenting

You Will Need

Karate panda if available or just yourselves!

Chalk

Instructions

- Say a word to the children, e.g. chin.
- Standing in lots of space(!), choose karate moves to chop up the word, for example a low front or side kick, a straight air punch or a defensive block!
- Say the phonemes which the word is made up of at the same time, ch-i-n.
- Segment to spell: write the word using crayons on large pieces of cardboard.

Threading Beads

You Will Need

Threading beads/buttons

String

Letter stamps

Paper

Instructions

- Thread beads/buttons onto a piece of string.
- Say a word to the children, e.g. stone.
- Move a bead along the string for each phoneme which you say in the word, s-t-o-n-e.
- Segment to spell: use letter stamps to spell the word.

Peg a Word

You Will Need

Pictures (you may want to add sound dots underneath)

Pegs

Magnetic letters

Instructions

- The child says the word in the picture, e.g. sheep.
- Say the word again but stretch it out.
- Clip a peg for each sound onto the picture, e.g. sh-ee-p.
- Segment to spell: make the word using magnetic letters.

Slinky Segmenting

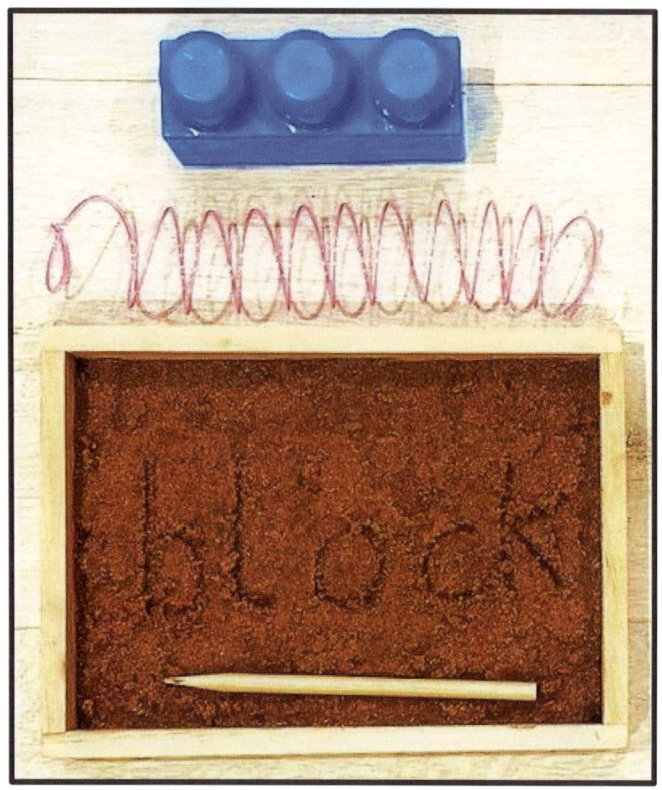

You Will Need

Slinky toy

Objects/pictures

Sand

Instructions

- Show the children an object or picture, e.g. a block.
- Use the slinky toy to stretch the word out slowly so that you can hear all of the sounds, b-l-o-ck.
- Repeat with different words.
- Segment to spell: write the words in damp sand.

Yoga Phonics

You Will Need

Yourselves!

Paper

Pens

Instructions

- Say a word to the children, e.g. drum.
- Perform a yoga stretch and at the same time, stretch the word to hear the sounds which make it, d-r-u-m.
- Repeat with different words.
- Segment to spell: write the words using felt pens.

Muffin Tin Segmenting

You Will Need

Muffin tin (or an egg carton will do)

Objects/pictures

Pom poms

Magnetic letters

Instructions

- Show the children an object, e.g. a pen.
- Place a pom pom in for each sound in the word, p-e-n.
- Repeat with different words.
- Segment to spell: make the word using magnetic letters.

Robot Voice

You Will Need

Toy robot (or just yourselves will do!)

Objects/pictures

Shaving foam

Tray

Instructions

- Show the children an object or a picture.
- Make the toy robot segment the word or pretend to be robots yourselves. Use your robot arms to break the word up into phonemes (one arm up/down at a time).
- Repeat with different words.
- Segment to spell: write the words in shaving foam.

Bubble Wrap Pop

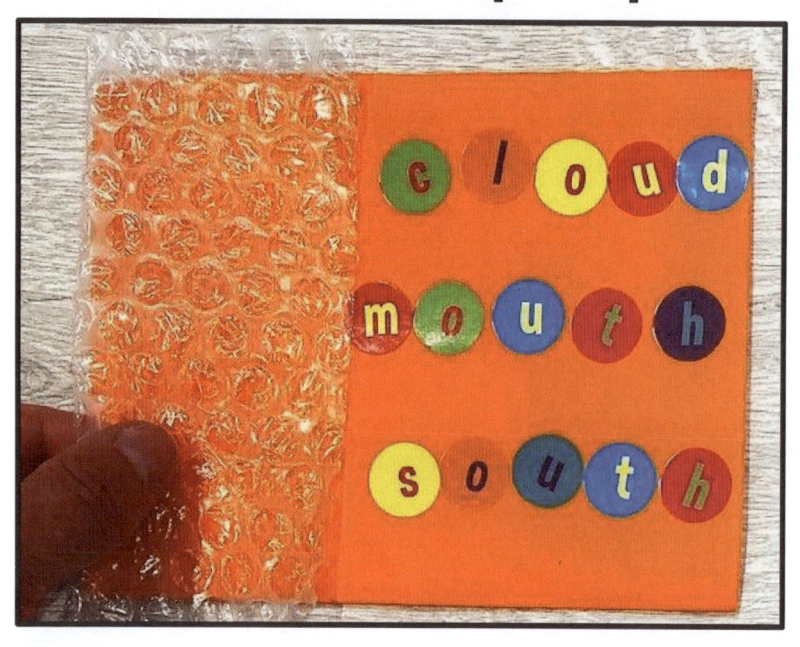

You Will Need

Bubble wrap/popper fidget toy

Alphabet stickers

Paper

Instructions

- Give each child a strip of bubble wrap.
- Say a word to the children, e.g. cloud.
- Ask the children to pop a bubble for each sound that they can hear in the word, c-l-ou-d.
- Repeat with different words.
- Segment to spell: spell the words using alphabet stickers on coloured paper.

Line Up Four

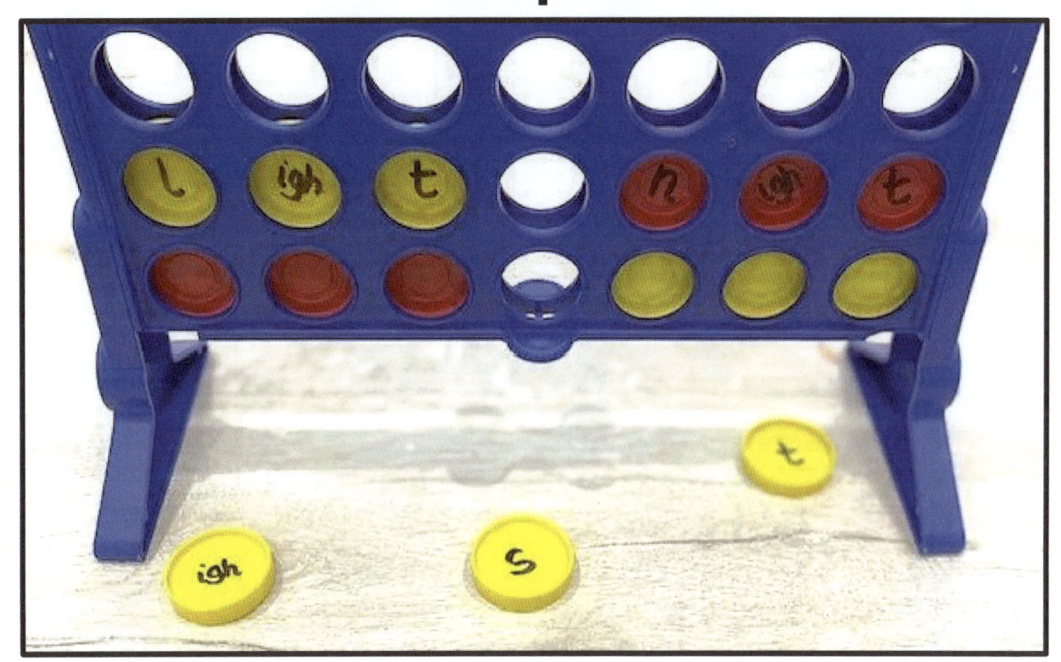

You Will Need

Line Up Four game

Pen

Instructions

- Say a word to the children, e.g. light.
- Ask the children to put a counter in for each sound that they can hear in the word and say the sounds out loud, l-igh-t.
- Repeat with different words.
- Segment to spell: write a grapheme on each counter. Provide the counters needed to spell a small selection of words.

I Spy

You Will Need

Telescope/binoculars (you could make your own from cardboard tubes if you don't have any!)

Toys

Light pad

Instructions

- Give one child a telescope.
- Ask them to spy at one of the toys. Can they pull apart the word and say its sounds?
- The other children guess which toy the child is spying on.
- Segment to spell: write the words on a light pad.

Balloon Rocket

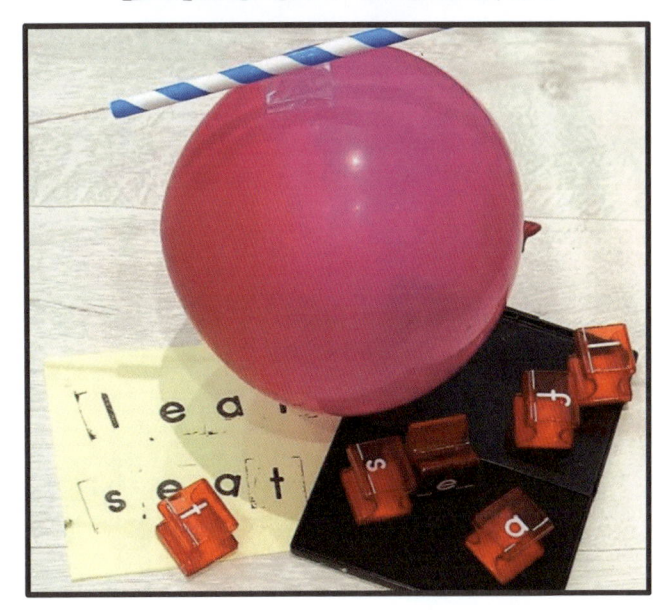

You Will Need
Balloon

String

Straw

Tape

Alphabet stamps & paper

Instructions
- Blow up a balloon and tape a straw to it, then thread the straw onto a piece of string.
- Give the children a word to segment.
- Segment the word as you let go of the balloon and it takes off along the string.
- Segment to spell: use alphabet stamps to spell the word.

Pass the Ball

You Will Need
Baton/ball

Whiteboard/easel & pen

Instructions
- 3/4/5 children to line up one behind the other.
- Say a word, e.g. a spoon.
- Ask the children to pass the ball backwards over their head (or between their legs), each saying a sound from the word, s-p-oo-n.
- Repeat with different words.
- Segment to spell: the last person in the line writes the word on a whiteboard/easel.

Hammering Words

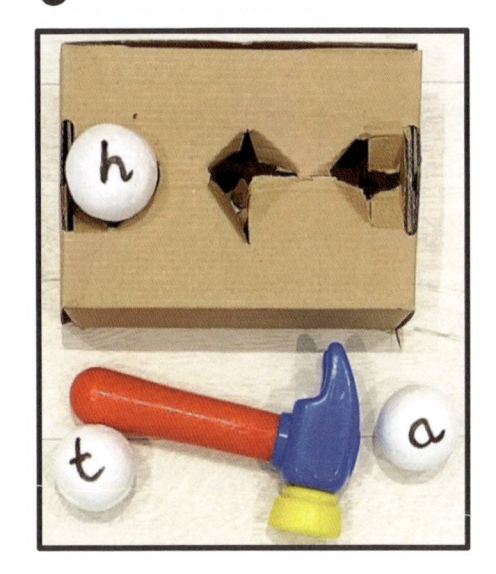

You Will Need

Cardboard box

Polystyrene balls

Toy hammer

Pen

Instructions

- Make 3 or 4 holes in the cardboard box, with small slits so that a polystyrene ball can be pushed through.
- Say a word to the children, e.g. hat.
- Hammer and say each sound in the word, h-a-t.
- Segment to spell: write graphemes on each ball. Can the children select and hammer the correct balls to spell the word?

The Floor is Lava!

You Will Need

Small mats/hoops to use as stepping stones

Grapheme flash cards

Instructions

- Say a word to the children, e.g. boy.
- Can the children safely jump from stepping stone to stepping stone to cross the lava? As they go, they should break the word into phonemes, b-oy.
- Repeat with different words.
- Segment to spell: ask children to place grapheme flash cards on the stepping stones to spell the word.

Stretch and Spell

You Will Need

Stretchy toy, e.g. Stretch Armstrong or Stretchkin (or slime to stretch, if you don't mind a bit of mess!)

Alphabet stamps

Paper

Instructions

- Say a word to the children, e.g. this.
- Use the toy's arms to stretch the word out slowly so that you can hear all of the sounds, th-i-s.
- Repeat with different words.
- Segment to spell: make the words using letter stamps.

Yo Yo Fun

You Will Need

Yo yo

Paintbrush & water

Instructions

- Say a word to the children, e.g. bath.
- As the children release their yo yos, they should segment the word into its phonemes, b-a-th.
- As the yo yo climbs back up the string, say the word again to check that you have used the correct sounds.
- Segment to spell: write the words using water and paintbrushes outside.
- *Take care with the long yo yo string and young children!*

Sloth Segmenting

You Will Need

Whiteboards

Pens

Instructions

- Say a word to the children, e.g. frog.
- Pretend to be sloths and stretch the word out very slowly so that you can hear all of the sounds, f-r-o-g.
- Repeat with different words.
- Segment to spell: write the words on whiteboards.
- *Alternatively, you could pretend to be tortoises or snails!*

Segmenting Bells

<u>You Will Need</u>

Bells

Chalkboards

Chalk

<u>Instructions</u>

- Say a word to the children, e.g. dog.
- Ask the children to ring a bell for each phoneme in the word, d-o-g.
- Repeat with different words.
- Segment to spell: record the words on chalkboards.
- *You could use little push lights instead for this activity.*

Ice Cream Phonics

You Will Need

Objects/pictures

Pictures of ice cream cones

Large pom poms

Scratchy notes

Instructions

- Show the children a toy, e.g. a pig.
- Place a scoop of ice cream (pom pom) onto the cones for each sound that you can hear in the word.
- Repeat with different toys.
- Segment to spell: write the words on scratchy notes.

Phonics Towers

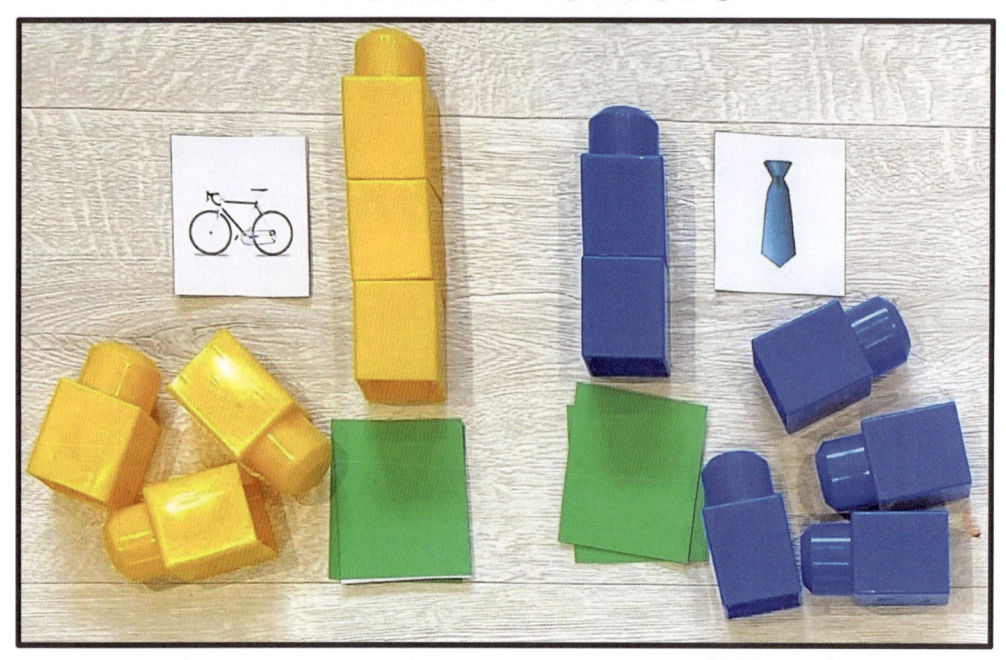

You Will Need

Pictures of objects to segment

Blocks

Whiteboards & pens

Instructions

- Give each pair of children 8/10 picture cards.
- Take turns to pick a card and turn it over.
- Use fingers to count the number of sounds which the word is made up of.
- Make a tower using that number of blocks.
- The person with the tallest tower at the end wins!
- Segment to spell: write the words on whiteboards.

Soar with Segmenting

You Will Need

Toy aeroplane/rocket

Large piece of paper/wallpaper

Pens/pencils

Instructions

- Say a word to the children, e.g. fan.
- Ask the children to make their toy plane/rocket take off. Say the sounds in the word as it goes, f-a-n.
- Repeat with different words.
- Segment to spell: write the words on a large piece of paper.

Slide and Segment

You Will Need

Picture of a slide/toy slide/real slide

Clipboard

Paper & pens

Instructions

- Say a word to the children, e.g. day.
- Ask the children to send a toy or go down a slide themselves, splitting the word into its phonemes as they go, d-ay.
- Repeat with different words.
- Segment to spell: write the words on a clipboard.

Segmenting Sticks

You Will Need

2 Sticks/rhythm sticks/claves per child

Flash cards

Washing line

Instructions

- Say a word to the children, e.g. pan.
- Ask the children to hit their sticks together and segment the word, p-a-n.
- Repeat with different words.
- Segment to spell: make the word using flashcards on a washing line.

TRICKY WORD TIPS & SPELLING ACTIVITIES

Tricky Word Spelling Tips

- TRICKY WORDS are also known as common exception or irregular words.
- They are used often in reading and writing.
- Tricky words contain letter-sound correspondences which the children have yet to learn, for example, 'was'. The 'a' corresponds to the phoneme /o/ which is unusual for children who are just beginning to learn to spell.
- With tricky words, focus on the sounds which children know first and then look carefully at the tricky part.
- Highlight the tricky part of the word using a different coloured pen or a highlighter. Alternatively, you could underline the tricky part.
- If there are other words with the same tricky pattern, then it makes sense to teach these at the same time, e.g. he, she, we, be or would, should, could.
- You could encourage the child to draw a picture in the tricky part of the word, to make it easier to remember.
- The tricky words and order in which they are taught will vary from school to school. Refer to the scheme used in your (child's) school and then use the following activities to supplement your spelling work.

Tricky Word Making

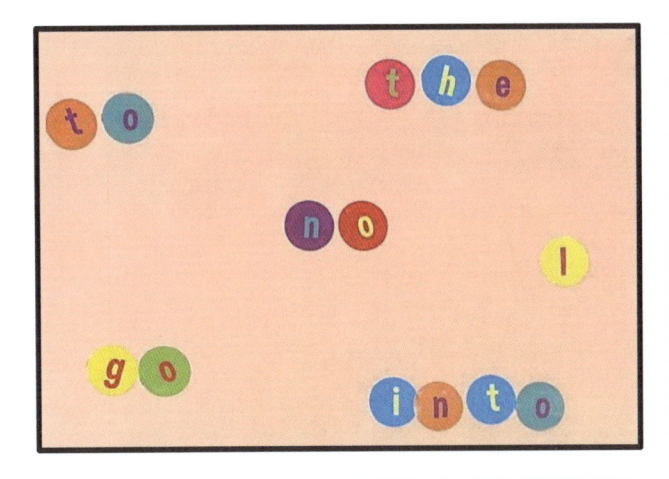

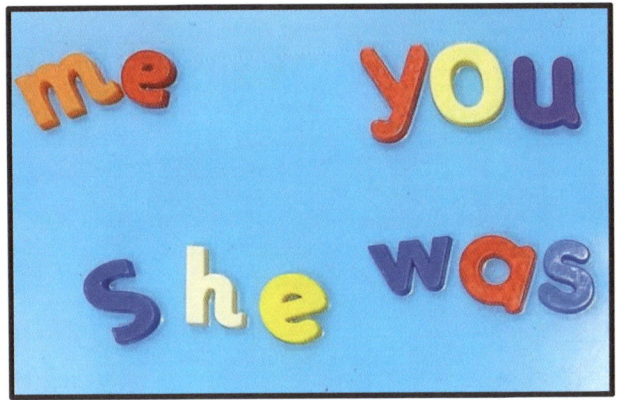

Children can build tricky words using fun visuals such as:

- Alphabet stickers on colourful paper
- By cutting letters out of comics and assembling them to make tricky word collages
- Using magnetic or wooden letters
- Using Scrabble letters
- Using grapheme flashcards

Tricky Word Making

Use a tactile approach to build tricky words:

- By rolling playdough to form the letters
- By arranging small blocks to make each of the letters
- By arranging loose parts such as shells, beads, buttons, etc. over each of the letters in the tricky word

Tricky Word Making

Practice building tricky words:

- By typing them out on a real or cardboard keyboard
- With blocks that have graphemes written on them
- By clipping grapheme pegs onto tricky word lolly pop sticks – write the word on the lolly pop stick and then each grapheme in the word onto separate pegs

Tricky Word Art

Make tricky word art by:

- Doing rainbow writing – use felt pens or crayons to write over the word in lots of different colours
- Writing the tricky word in white crayon and then using watercolour paints to reveal it
- Writing the tricky word on a big piece of paper and decorating with feathers, felt and other collage materials

Tricky Word Art

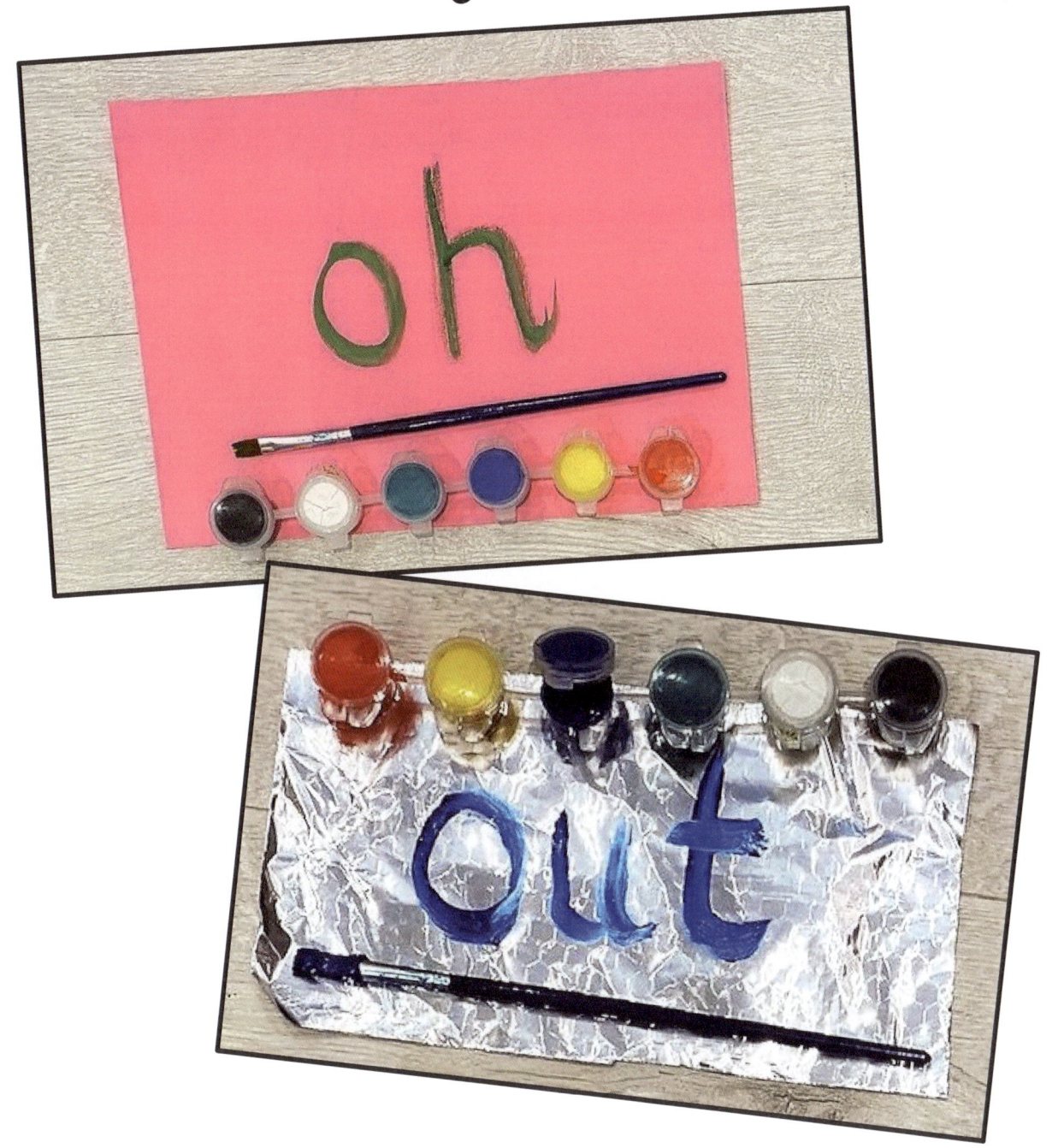

Make tricky word art by:

- Painting tricky words on paper
- Painting tricky words on foil

Tricky Word Art

Make tricky word art more visual by:

- Spelling the words in squiggle, bubble or fancy writing
- Asking children to draw shapes around the spellings to help them to remember the words

Tricky Word Writing

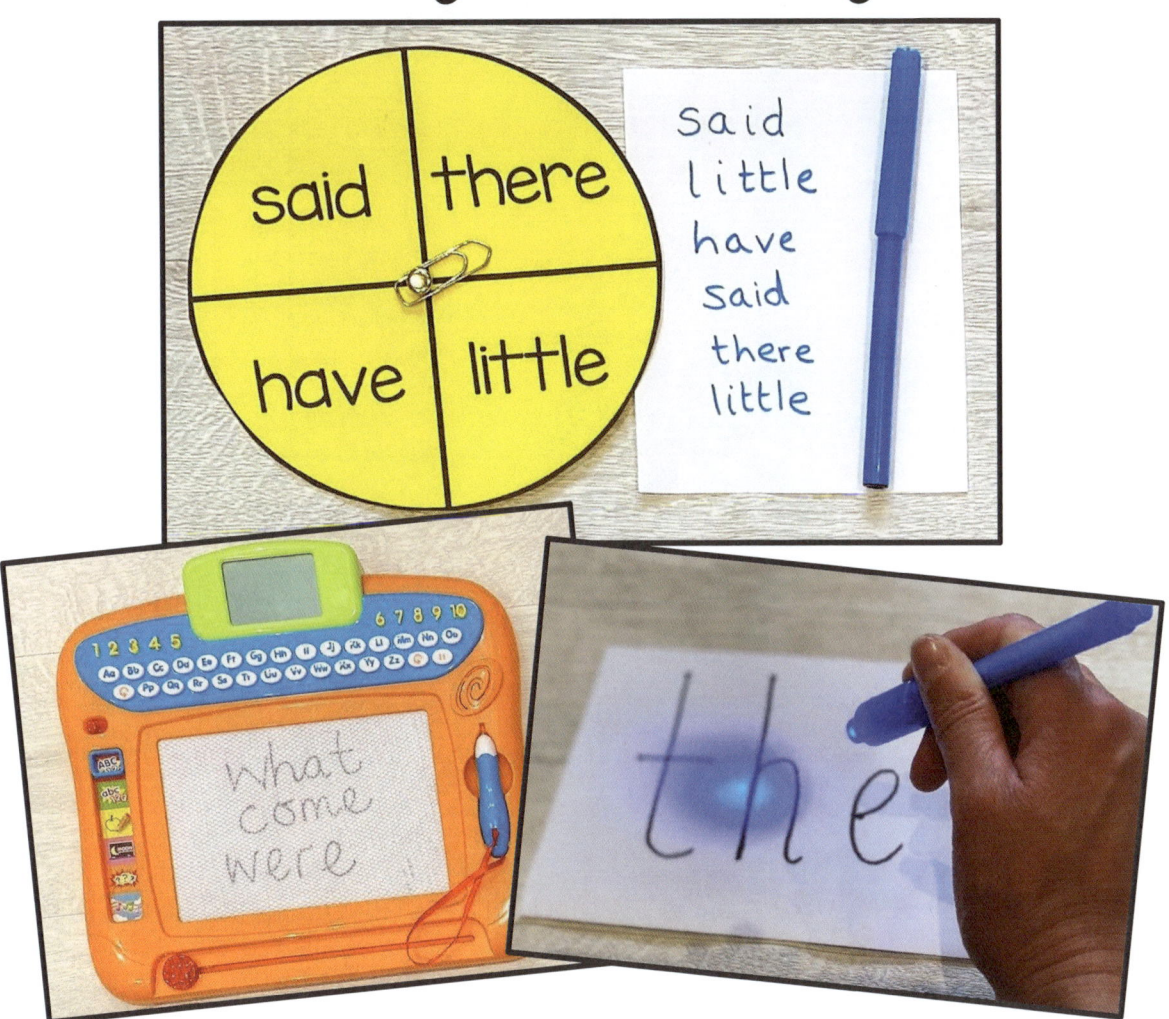

Make writing tricky words more fun by:

- Making a spinner using a circle of card, a split pin and a paper clip. Write tricky words on the spinner and then spell the word which you land on
- Writing them on whiteboards or an etcha-sketch
- Writing the words with your finger in the sky
- 'Tracing' over the letters with a magic spy pen

Tricky Word Writing

Practice spelling tricky words:

- By tracing over tricky word flash cards with tracing paper and pens or pencils
- By seeing how many times you can write the tricky word before a sand timer runs out
- Using a wooden stylus to write them on scratchy notes (matte black surface which scratches off to reveal a rainbow background)

Tricky Word Writing

Practice spelling tricky words on a variety of different writing surfaces, such as:

- Using chalk on the ground
- Using a feather, paintbrush or finger in sand/glitter/oats
- Using a stick to write the words in mud

Tricky Word Activities

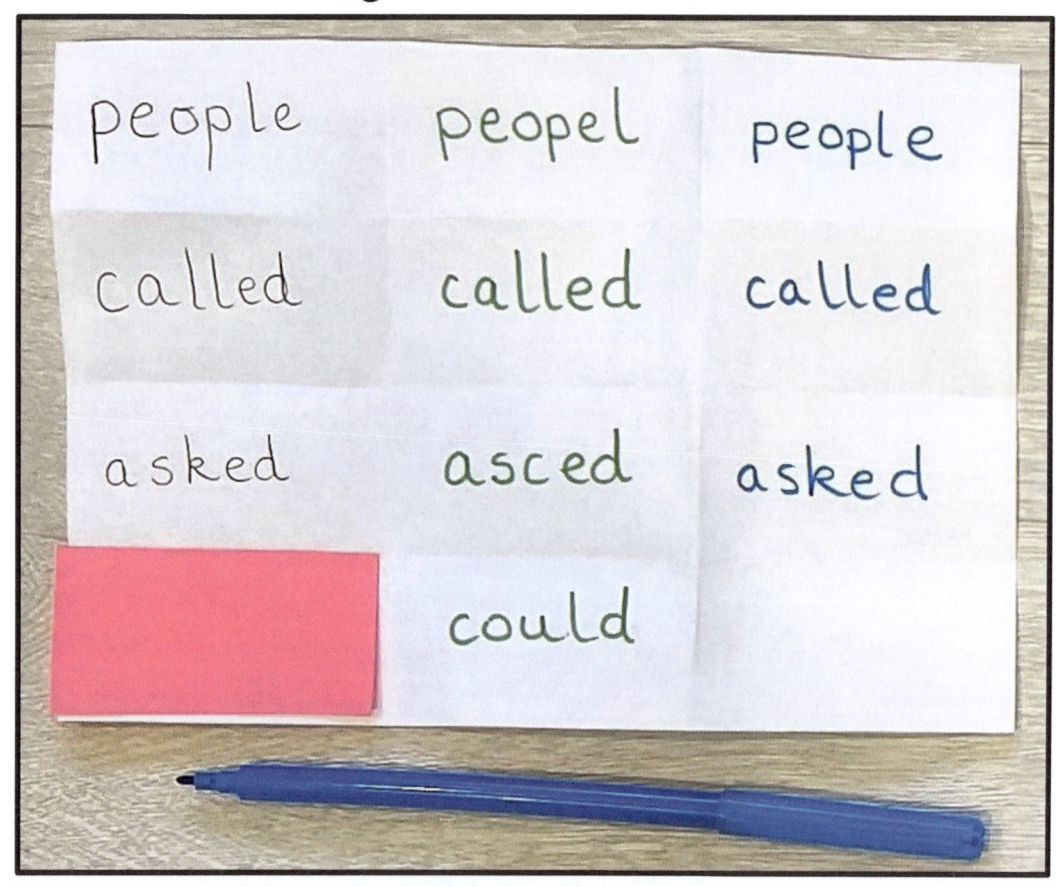

Look Trace Say Cover Write Check

- Write each of the focus tricky words in the first column
- Children look at the first word and trace over it with a finger, saying the letters at the same time
- They should cover the word up and write it without peeping, then check that they have spelled the word correctly
- Cover the word and write it again in the final column
- Repeat until the child has practiced spelling all of the tricky words on the sheet

Tricky Word Activities

Roll and Spell

- Create a 6 x 5 grid
- Write the tricky words which you are focussing on in the first column, with 1-6 dots next to each one
- Children roll a dice and write the corresponding word in the next box along
- Repeat until all of the boxes are filled

Tricky Word Activities

Tricky Word Picture

- Look carefully at the sounds which the child knows and then at the tricky parts of the word
- Ask the child to take a 'photo' of the word, using a real or imaginary camera
- Can they keep the word in their 'mind's eye' and remember the part which is tricky?

Tricky Word Activities

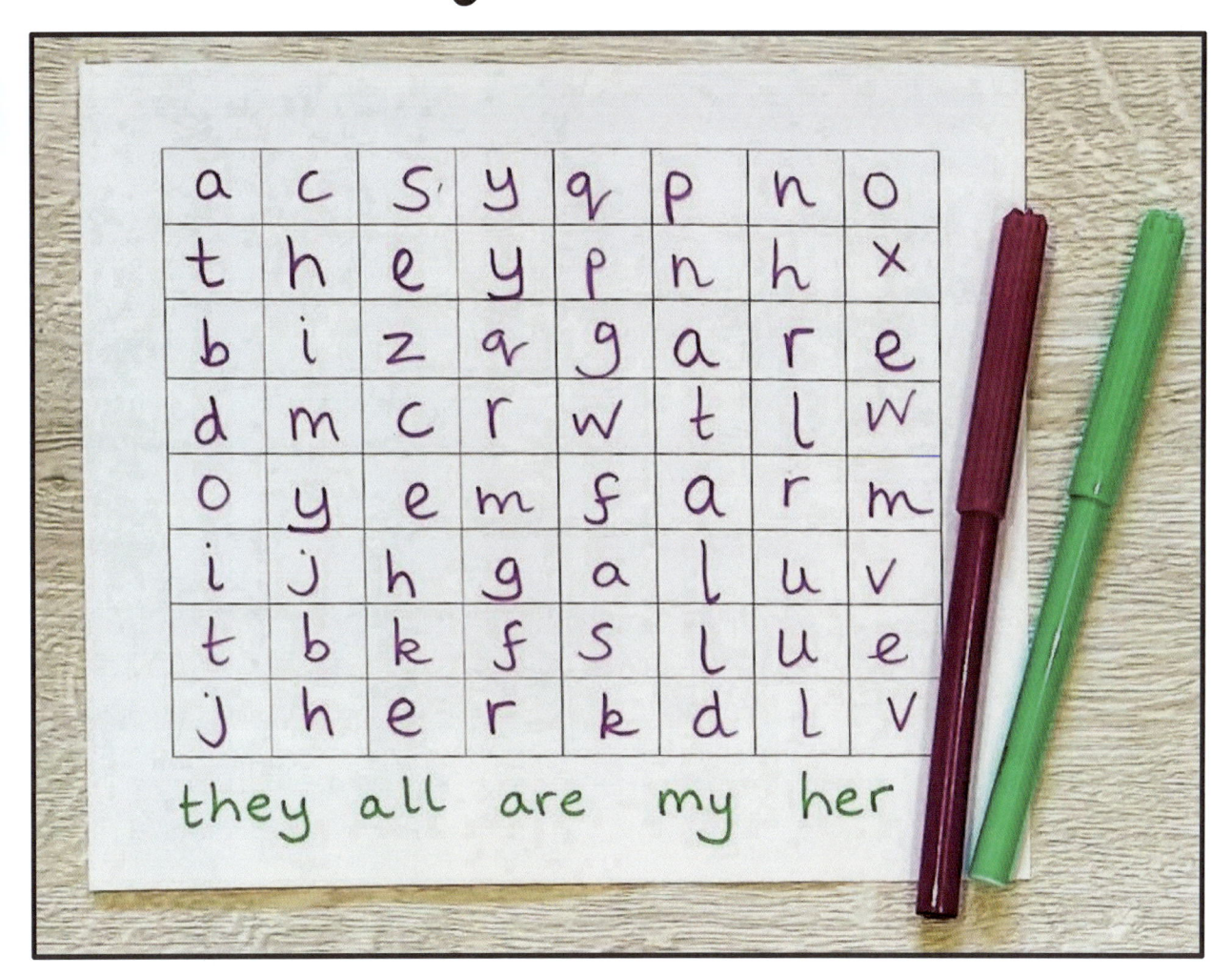

Tricky Words Wordsearch

- Give each child a blank grid
- Give them the focus tricky words to write at the bottom
- Ask the children to write the words horizontally or vertically on their grid and to then hide them by writing other letters in the remaining boxes
- The children can swap wordsearches and hunt for each other's hidden words

Tricky Word Activities

Spy Spellings

- Ask the children to write their tricky words using an invisible ink pen
- Can they use the UV light in the pen to reveal the words?
- Shine the light on the easy parts and then the tricky part

Tricky Word Activities

Tricky Word Stairs

- Draw some steps going down a piece of paper
- Write the first letter in the tricky word inside the first step, e.g. 'l' for the first letter in 'little'
- Write the first and second letters in the word on the second step
- Continue adding another letter in the word on each new step, until the whole word has been written

Author's Note

Thank you for reading my book. I hope that you have found the activities useful and that they have brought your little learners on in leaps and bounds!

If you loved the book and have a spare minute, I would really appreciate a short review on Amazon. As a new author, your help in spreading the word is greatly appreciated.

Thank you!
No Worksheets Allowed

You might also be interested in:

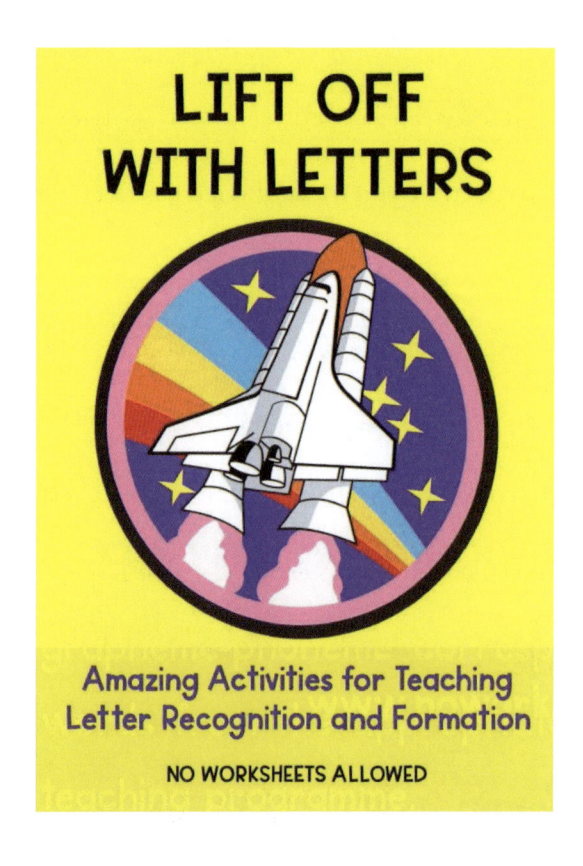

LIFT OFF WITH LETTERS
Amazing Activities for Teaching Letter Recognition and Formation
NO WORKSHEETS ALLOWED

BLAST OFF WITH BLENDING
36 Awesome Activities for Teaching Children to Read
NO WORKSHEETS ALLOWED

Printed in Great Britain
by Amazon